THE GAP

Bridge The Space Between
Where You Are And Where You Want To Be

Brigitte Van Tuijl

ISBN Paperback: 978-90-830654-2-7
ISBN e-book: 978-90-830654-3-4

Visit www.booksbybrigitte.com for more books by the author.
Visit www.gapbookgift.com for additional gifts.

The information provided in this book is designed to inspire, educate, motivate, and enlighten you on the subjects discussed. It's not meant as a substitute for professional coaching or other expert assistance. If such level of assistance is required, please seek the services of a competent professional or contact the author directly for one-to-one coaching options. The author assumes no liability for use of the information and exercises.

Cover Design by Susan D. Johnson
Interior Design by FormattedBooks.com

Also by Brigitte van Tuijl

Ontdek Wat Je Écht Wilt En Maak Daar (Je) Werk Van

*Unmute Your Life - break free from fear & go
for what you REALLY want*

CONTENTS

INTRODUCTION

Realizing dreams, completing big projects, or making big changes is not always easy. It's hard to be in the gap, the in-between phase: the new isn't here yet, and you're already done with the old. You know where you want to be, you long for it . . . but you're not there yet. Waiting can be hard, especially if it takes a long time before you see your dream come true in real life.

This gap is always present regardless of what your dream or project is. I'm sure you've experienced the gap before. I've experienced it many times myself. There was a four-year period between *knowing* I wanted to start my business and *starting* it. I needed a year and a half of training before I was ready to take on my first client as a coach. And most recently, it took me nine (nine!) years to write and publish my book *Unmute Your Life - break free from fear & go for what you REALLY want*. That nine-year gap* was an especially frustrating one. :-) You'd think this nine-year period inspired me to write this book, but I had the idea for it before I wrote *Unmute Your Life*. I made the first notes, which contained an almost complete outline of this book, in 2011. After I started coaching in 2002, I could see my clients struggle with wanting something and not having it. The wait triggered impatience, frustration, insecurities, and fears. I doled out the same advice over and over and thought it would be a good idea to put it all in a book one day.

It took a while before that day came. Other projects came first. But here it is. Apparently, now is the right time for it. And you can use this book now, for whatever project or dream you're working on.

Part One takes you through three essential stages in bridging the gap: letting go of the old, embracing the new, and being present in the now. These stages are not necessarily chronological. Being present in the now serves you always, in everything you do. The process of releasing the old and embracing the new can come up several times during your journey—sometimes even daily. And embracing the new is something you can practice until it becomes your new normal. By that time, there are *new* new things to embrace and play with.

Part Two gives you additional tips and inspiration to stay motivated while you work toward your goals.

Whatever you're working on and no matter how long it takes you to manifest it, this book helps you move through your journey with as much ease and joy as possible. You may still feel frustrated at times, pissed off at how long it takes, or annoyed that you haven't achieved your goal yet. You're human and those feelings are normal! Allow yourself to feel whatever you feel and to complain, bitch, or vent if you need it. Better out than in. :-) After that, just pick up this book and read whatever chapter speaks to you then. And you'll feel better in no time.

I wish you a wonderful, joyous journey! May this book help you stay motivated and encouraged so you will see your beautiful dreams and creations come to life, regardless of how long it takes.

Love,

Brigitte

---

*I'm grateful it took so long, though! I learned a lot from this nine-year writing journey and am very grateful for it. I share why it took so long and all that I learned in a PDF you receive when you sign up for free book gifts at www.gapbookgift.com. The information on the PDF provides some additional inspiration and encouragement to never give up—it helps you see that if you just keep at it, one day *your* dream will come true, too!

PART ONE:

RELEASE THE OLD,
EMBRACE THE NEW,
BE PRESENT IN THIS MOMENT

CHAPTER 1:

Make Peace with the Past

You need to make peace with the past if you carry around past disappointments. Based on your past experiences, you may feel resentment, anger, frustration, a lack of trust, or impatience about your goal. When you're hesitant to do something because it didn't work out before, you may ask yourself, why would it work now? Thoughts and feelings like these are in your way. If that's the case for you, it's important to make peace with the past. Here's how you can do that.

Step one: give space to your emotions

Let out your emotions about your past experiences. Vent, rage, complain, cry. Do whatever you need to get it out of your system.

You don't have to go *looking* for those emotions. They're present or they're not, and you already feel them when they are. If they are present, it's important to allow yourself to fully *feel* and *release* your feelings.

Don't judge yourself—it's okay to feel what you feel.

Most importantly: don't suppress your emotions! That always backfires. Emotions you try to deny or hold back are never really gone. They're just lurking in the shadows, waiting to come out in full force at a later time. Often you can feel them as a low, dull sensation somewhere in the background throughout the day. They color your mood, your actions, AND the results of your work—and not in a good way. So whatever emotions you need to release: set them free!

Step two: give space to your thoughts

After you release what you *feel* about your past actions or results, it's time to release your *thoughts* about them, too. How? By writing them down. All of them.

- What do you think about your past actions or results?
- What stories do you tell yourself about them?
- What meaning do you give them?
- What do you think your past result tells you about yourself?
- What do you think it tells you about your business?
- What do you think it tells you about your chance of realizing your new project or dream?

Write down all your thoughts exactly as they come to you. Don't filter, judge, or criticize anything. Be open and curious to see what's going on in your mind, or, to be more precise, what your inner critic has to say.

You don't have to do anything with what you write down. You are able to release your thoughts just by putting them down on paper.

Step three: give space to your soul

You know what your mind is telling you. You just wrote it all down. And as you can probably see, most of it is negative. Your thoughts are colored by fears and doubts and by what your inner critic thinks of you and your actions. The result is negative stories and beliefs that make it hard to move forward with excitement and joy. This negativity makes it difficult to believe you can get what you want, which makes it harder to take action. Staying where you are or giving up becomes more attractive. None of this is helpful.

What you need is a fresh perspective. A higher perspective. The perspective of your soul. Or, if that concept is too vague for you, the perspective of your wise inner being. You already know what your inner critic has to say. Now let your inner wise one shine her light on your past. You can gain this higher perspective by answering the following questions.

- What have you learned from your journey from where you were to where you are now?
- What is possible for you because of that journey?
- What gift have you received from the journey?
- What opportunities are now available for you?
- How have you grown because of this experience?
- How have you healed?

- How did you become stronger because of what happened?
- Is there anything else that comes up when you ask your soul what message she has for you now?

Write everything down, even when it sounds unrealistic, weird, or untrue. This exercise is about finding a new perspective that will allow you to move forward with faith and joy, and is about shifting your energy and your mood. As a result, you'll feel better AND make space for better results.

Step four: release and move on

Look at everything you wrote down.

- What thoughts, habits, and beliefs (still) serve you? Which of these will you take with you into the future?
- Which of these thoughts, habits, and beliefs no longer serve you?
- Which ones will you leave behind?

Burn or shred the paper(s) or delete the document(s) with your negative thoughts from steps one and two. Hold on to the paper from step three with the perspective from your soul, if you like. You may want to read through that again later. You don't have to, though. If it feels better to throw that out, too, do that!

When you've finished this exercise, you will have let go of the old and made space for the new. Sometimes negative thoughts come up again at a later stage. If so, you can do this exercise again. Or go straight to the perspective from your soul. Do whatever you need to allow yourself to feel what you feel and release your feelings, too! It's never a good idea to suppress your emotions. Always acknowledge them and allow yourself to feel them. That's the best way to set them free so they don't bother you or hold you back.

REFLECTION

Is there something in your past that still triggers emotions or strong feelings in you today?

How would you feel if those feelings no longer bothered you?

What possibilities or opportunities would not feeling those things open for you?

CHAPTER 2:
Release Habits & Actions That No Longer Serve You

Your current habits and patterns brought you to where you are today. Some of them are still helpful. Others no longer serve you. And when you're honest with yourself, you already know what you need to let go of and what you need to do more of . . .

What habits no longer serve you?

Write them all down. Once your list feels complete, look at all the items on your list and identify your most unhelpful habit. Which one holds you back the most?

What new habit(s) will help you realize your dream or complete your project?

Write them all down. Once this list feels complete, determine what the most helpful new habit could be. Which one will serve you best? Pick the one that will have the biggest positive impact to help you achieve your goal.

How will you implement your new habit?

Just thinking about your new habit won't make a difference. Come up with a concrete, practical way you can benefit from integrating this new routine into your life. Here's an example of what that can look like. Maybe your dream is to write your first book. The most helpful habit you can think of is to write every day. You decide to write 1,000 words every day, right after you finish drinking your morning coffee. You still have to actually DO it, but at least you've identified a concrete action to help you work toward writing your book.

Maybe your new helpful habit is to meditate. Great! Determine how, when, and how often you will do this. Thinking about these details upfront makes it easier to actually practice your new habit, helping you to continue doing it until you no longer need it or it becomes one of your default habits.

REFLECTION

What habits or actions no longer work for you? (If any.)

What one to three (new) habits or actions will bring you closer to your goals?

CHAPTER 3:
Gratitude

Feeling grateful is a powerful manifestation tool. Gratefulness enhances your well-being and improves your mood AND it helps you receive and notice more things to feel grateful for. Gratitude gives you extra energy and opens you up to receive even more beauty and goodness in your life. It also makes you realize how much you have to be grateful for and how good your life already is. It's okay to still want more—but feeling grateful for what you already have helps you enjoy your journey and keeps impatience away. Or at least, helps you feel *less* impatient.

The easiest way to use the power of gratefulness is to write down, every day, at least five things you feel grateful for. The key here is to really FEEL grateful. Just going through the motions and writing down some random stuff without feeling thankful won't do you much good.

It's okay to repeat the same things every day. As long as you feel genuine appreciation, you can continue to write the same things.

Also, make it a habit to feel appreciation for good things that happen throughout the day. When someone gives you a compliment, don't brush it off. Consciously receive it and let it sink in for a moment. When something makes you happy, really soak up that happy feeling and give thanks to whomever or whatever made you happy. Thank the sun for beautiful sunsets, thank the universe for cloudless skies, thank the moon for lighting up the dark. Consciously take in whatever delights you and brings you joy and throw in a little "Thank you!" as well. You don't have to say it out loud, but do so if that makes you feel good!

One last way to play with gratitude is to feel grateful for something *before* you've received it. Just assume you will get it and give thanks in advance. Let go of feeling attached to the if, how, and when you will receive it, though! Attachment keeps what you want away from you. Letting go of attachment opens you up, allowing you to receive what you want—or something infinitely better.

REFLECTION

What three things do you feel grateful for in this moment?

What's already good in your personal life?

What's already good in your business?

CHAPTER 4:
Prepare for Pitfalls

No matter how much you love your goal, project, or dream, there can be times when you lose touch with your excitement. Times when you self-sabotage or procrastinate or even give up. There's nothing wrong with that. And nothing is lost when you procrastinate or self-sabotage for a while. You can always get back on track. But these times *can* make your journey harder than it needs to be.

A powerful way to make achieving your goal easier and to prevent yourself from stepping into any pitfalls is by preparing for them.

You know yourself. You know when things can get hard for you. You know at what point you can lose motivation or lose momentum. You may have to think about it for a bit, but you *know*. So let's think about it now. Because once you're clear on the ways you might give up or the times when it might become difficult for you, you can come up with ways to prevent yourself falling into those pitfalls. All you have to do is to answer these questions.

- At what point might you give up or start self-sabotaging?
- Under what circumstances could that happen?
- What things might be triggers and make you want to give up?
- How can you recognize that you are starting to sabotage yourself?
- What can you do to prevent the problem?

For me, for example, impatience is a big pitfall. I want to see results FAST. When that doesn't happen, I lose my focus and motivation. I can recognize this is happening when my initial excitement starts to fade and when I start to feel rushed.

I can prevent this by bringing my focus to why my dream or goal truly matters to me. I remind myself of the deeper reason I want this. Another thing that helps me is being present and enjoying each moment as much as I can. When I enjoy my days as much as I possibly can, I'm not bothered by how quickly or slowly things go. I'm just enjoying my time.

REFLECTION

What are your pitfalls?

How you can prevent yourself from stepping into them?

CHAPTER 5:
Literally Make Space

Releasing beliefs and habits that no longer serve you creates emotional, mental, and spiritual space to receive something different. Clearing up your *physical* environment creates space for your dreams to come true, too. Not because you need more literal space (some dreams or goals do, but most don't), but because cleaning up actual stuff helps to open up your heart and mind. Tidying shifts something inside you and opens you up to be able to receive something new. Clearing clutter makes space to receive more on all levels.

So, how do you know what stuff to get rid of? Don't worry, I'm not asking you to clear out every inch of your house from attic to basement. I have a simpler, smaller, and definitely quicker way to make space for your dreams. All you have to do is read through the questions below and pay attention to what comes up while you read. Then throw out whatever came to mind.

- What in your home or office keeps you tied to the past?
- What in your business stops you from moving forward?
- When you wonder what might be keeping you where you are, what else comes to mind?

Let go of whatever comes up. Notes, documents, stuff on your computer, things, pictures, books, clothes: throw them out, give them away, let them go. You don't have to do it all at once. If a lot came up, you can do it step-by-step. And if you feel you're still attached to it and aren't ready to part from it, ask yourself what exactly it is you want to hold on to. Often, it's not the thing itself but something else completely. An old self-image, a memory, a feeling of comfort or safety. Whatever you try to hold on to, does it really still serve you? And if yes, can you give this to yourself in another way?

I remember cleaning up my computer years ago and going through a bunch of online programs I had bought. Some were easy to throw away, because I was certain I no longer needed them. There were a few I could not say good-bye to but not because I thought I would use them again. So I asked myself what I was really holding on to. I realized then that I felt insecure about my qualities as an entrepreneur. I felt I didn't know enough and wasn't doing a good enough job. Keeping those online programs on building a business gave me confidence. Maybe I didn't know enough, but thankfully I had the information I needed at my fingertips! I realized I would never use the content of these programs, though—they were filled with cookie-cutter recipes that didn't feel right for me. The solution to my insecurity was not to hold on to these programs but to find other ways to feel confident.

REFLECTION

What items are you holding on to that keep you tied to the past?

Let go of them. You'll be surprised at how much space and breathing room this gives you.

CHAPTER 6:

Who You Need to Be—
The New You

The person you are now brought you to where you are today. This is as far as she can take you. To reach a new level, you need to tap into a new level of yourself. You need to become an expanded version of yourself to create an expanded version of your business and life. That person is already part of you. You can connect with her right now. And the way you do that is by getting clear on who she is first, and by acting as her next.

Start by describing who you need to be to achieve your (new) project or goal. These questions help you paint the picture of this next-level version of yourself.

- What does the person who already realized your dream believe?
- What habits did she let go of?
- What negative thoughts are no longer going through her mind?
- What does she no longer doubt or worry about?

- What are her expectations about the actions she takes?
- How does she feel about herself, her goals, and her life? Why?
- How does she take care of herself?
- What's her most powerful habit?
- How does she move through her days?
- How does she act when she encounters a problem?
- What is she no longer doing?
- What does she no longer allow?
- Anything else comes to mind?

Once you know who you need to be, close your eyes. See this new version of yourself before you. Imagine that she is already you, right now. *Feel* how it feels to be her. Feel it in your body. Notice your energy. Notice your posture.

Now that you know what it's like to be her, you can consciously step into your next-level self every day. Simply close your eyes, take on her posture, think about who she is and how she is, and *feel* it in your body. Then open your eyes and move through your day with this energy.

REFLECTION

What's the biggest difference between the new you and the current you?

What becomes possible for you and your business if you act like you're the new you?

How will your business and life be different?

CHAPTER 7:

Act as the New You

In the previous chapter, you identified what the next-level version of yourself looks like. You learned how to tap into her energy and *be* her.

Now that you know this, you can take the next step: to act like her. You do that by answering questions like these and implementing your answers.

- What would the new you do today?
- How would she handle the current situation you're facing at work?
- What decision would she make if she were faced with the issue you have in your business?
- How would she handle the project you're working on?
- What would she eat?
- What would she wear?
- How would she spend her evenings?
- What would she focus on today?
- And what would she definitely NOT spend any time on?

REFLECTION

What would the new you do today?

What would she do *right now*?

CHAPTER 8:

Act from Where You Want to Be, Not from Where You Are

Acting from where you want to be is similar to what I described in the previous chapter, *Act as the New You*. It's a different way of getting clarity on your next best action or decision.

Here's an example to show you what it means to act from where you want to be, instead of acting from where you are. Imagine that it's your goal to work with international clients. Right now, you offer your services to clients only from The Netherlands, and you work in Dutch. Acting from where you are means that you continue offering your services only in Dutch, your website is available only in Dutch, and your social media updates are written only in Dutch.

Acting from where you want to be looks different. For example, you translate your website into English, so people can choose between reading it in English or Dutch. You write Facebook updates in English. You create a new workshop in English. That's acting from where you want to be.

Ask yourself questions like, what can I do to get closer to my goal? What changes can I make that will bring me closer to my dream? Is something holding me back from making these changes and if so, what can I do to move forward anyway? What's an easy step I can take today that brings me a little bit closer to my goal? The answers to those questions show you how you can act from where you want to be.

REFLECTION

In what ways are you still acting from where you currently are?

How could you act from where you *want* to be?

If you trusted that achieving your goal was a done deal and nothing could go wrong, what would you do now and how would you act?

CHAPTER 9:

Act as if You Already Have It

Acting as if you already have it is similar to acting from where you want to be. Here's an example of what that can look like.

Let's say you're single, but you long for a new partner. What you can do is imagine that (s)he is already in your life. Set the table for two instead of just for one. Buy a double bed if you don't have one. Clear out a drawer for their socks and underwear.

Or, to give a business-related example, let's say you want to make an impact on the lives of thousands of people. But right now you only have fifty-five likes on Facebook. Show up to work as if you already have 55,000 likes. Write as if all 55,000 people read your updates. When you do a Facebook Live, imagine that you're talking to 55,000 people.

REFLECTION

If you already had everything you desired, what would you do today?

If you already had everything you ever wanted, how would you act and how would you show up?

CHAPTER 10:

What Do You Need to Believe?

Your mindset plays a crucial role in what you do, how you feel, and the results you see in your business and life. The mindset that you have now brought you to where you are today. Your new level, however, requires you to level up your mindset. Plus, having the right mindset will help you *be* and *act* as the next-level version of yourself.

Here's how you can upgrade your mindset and anchor these new beliefs so they start to feel normal to you. First, answer these questions to make a list of what you need to believe to realize your dream or achieve your goal.

- What do you need to believe about yourself?
- What do you need to believe about your dream?
- What do you need to believe about others?
- What do you need to believe about the world?
- Anything else you need to believe?

After you've made that list, move on to the next step: explore areas where you can see that this belief is already true. Maybe you can see evidence of it in your own life, in the past or in the present. Or maybe you can see evidence of it in the lives of others. It doesn't matter *where* you see it or *when* it showed up. All that matters is that you *see* it.

The evidence is ALWAYS there, because we live in a world of duality: for every dark there is light, for every wrong there is a right. These things always coexist. It's just a matter of what you focus on: the light? Or the dark? The good? Or the bad? The wrong? Or the right? Do you focus on what's already here? Or what you think you still lack?

When you don't consciously steer your thoughts in a certain direction, your mind actively searches for what's scary or what could go wrong. That's because your mind tries to keep you safe and is always on the lookout for danger. Plus, we live in a world that's overly focused on fears and bad stuff. Just pick up a mainstream newspaper or watch the news, and you'll see exactly what I mean. We're bombarded with negative shit all day, every day, so it takes conscious practice (and an awareness of what we feed our mind) to keep a positive outlook on our goals, our dreams, and our lives.

Mind you, I'm not saying you should overlook the bad or pretend nothing is ever wrong. Ignoring these things is like taking a bypass—a way to skirt around something you don't want to acknowledge. Bypassing the hard things doesn't serve you. On the contrary! It only causes you to bottle up your emotions until you either explode or have a nervous breakdown. Not a good idea. Some things are wrong and need to be acknowledged and changed. Some things are painful and need to be felt to be healed. What I mean by looking for positive evidence as a way to steer your mind in a positive direction is to create a mindset of power and possibilities. A mindset that serves you instead of a mindset that holds you back and makes you feel like crap. Let me give you some examples of how to look for positive evidence.

Let's say that one thing you need to believe is that you're capable of handling everything that comes your way. It's easy to come up with examples of situations where you *didn't* know what to do or say. You're human, and we all have moments like these. But there are ALSO moments that prove you knew *exactly* what to do, and that you did it perfectly. Those are the moments we're looking for. Think back and come up with three (or more) examples. Maybe someone offended your friend, and you stood up for her. Maybe your tire burst on the highway, and you safely steered the car into the emergency lane. Maybe you were able to turn a problem into a business opportunity.

Or maybe you need to believe that other people are interested in what you offer. Maybe a client told you how happy she was with your coaching. Maybe someone asked you when your next workshop will be. Or maybe someone signed up for your newsletter last month. These are all signs people are interested in your business and work.

What if you need to believe something you haven't experienced yet? That's okay. Seeing evidence of it in other people's lives means it's possible in general. Which makes it possible for you, too! Maybe you're looking for your dream home but aren't sure you can find something within your budget. Do you have a friend or family member who found a house in a weird, coincidental way, or for much cheaper than they expected? Did you ever hear or read a story like that? It's likely that you have. If you can't find any examples of houses, then think about other examples where you received something you never thought you would get. Did you ever buy something at an unexpected bargain? Did you ever get something as an unexpected gift? Do you know or know of other people who experienced something like this? I bet you do!

Make sure you write down all the evidence of your new, positive beliefs. You can look at them whenever you need a little pick-me-up. And if you like, you can add fresh evidence the moment you encounter it, too. Seeing that list grow will give your mindset and expectations an even bigger boost.

REFLECTION

What if you already believed all your new supporting beliefs?

What would be different?

What would you do today?

How would you act?

CHAPTER 11:
Feel It

Close your eyes. Think about your goal or dream. Then imagine that you already *have* it. You've closed the gap and whatever it is you long or strive for: it's yours now! If you see any images before you, that's good. But if you see nothing, that's perfect, too. This is all about how it *feels*.

Forget about the *how*. Don't worry about the timing or other practicalities. All you have to do is notice how having the thing you want makes you feel. You don't have to visualize it or do anything else. Just FEEL. Stay with this feeling for as long as you like. Then open your eyes. Now take this feeling with you into the rest of your day.

Do this exercise regularly, as often as you like. You can do it first thing in the morning when you're still in bed, for example. Regular practice helps you realize your dream or goal with more ease. By practicing how it feels to have already realized it, you embody your dream. It starts to feel normal to have what you want, and you'll automatically and naturally start acting in ways that help you manifest your desires. Your energy is tuned into your goal—and this helps you achieve it with less effort.

Play with it! This is an easy and fun exercise that will benefit you greatly.

REFLECTION

How will accomplishing your dream make you feel?

Can you feel that feeling now?

CHAPTER 12:
Be Open & Curious

Be curious about what's next. Be open to how good life can get and how beautifully it can unfold. This is the best state of mind to be in to realize your dreams and achieve your most outrageous goals.

Being open and curious allows you to be your most creative self and to see opportunities and ideas as they come to you—and not just see them, but make the best use of them, too!

Curiosity is also a great antidote to worrying, overthinking, and fear. When you're worried, stressed, or scared, your mind and heart are closed. You have less access to your strengths, you don't see solutions, you can't hear your intuition, and you don't feel good, either. Curiosity helps you relax and open up again. You can easily shift into being more curious by changing your thoughts. Here are some examples to show you how that works.

Original thought "I don't know how to do this!"

New thought "I'm curious to see how this will work out."

Original thought "I don't think this is possible."

New thought "I wonder how this might happen!"

Original thought "This scares the crap out of me. I'm afraid to do this!"

New thought "I'm curious to see what's on the other side of this fear!"

Be curious about your journey. Don't focus on deadlines, assumptions, or expectations about how long it will take or how hard it will be. Open your heart and your mind by thinking thoughts like these instead.

- "I wonder how much fun I'll have along the way!?"
- "I can't wait to see the manifestation of this dream fall into place."
- "I wonder how easy it can be?"
- "I wonder how good it can get!?"

REFLECTION

If you were open and curious about your journey and how easy and fun it could be, what would excite you?

What could you do today to be more open and curious?

CHAPTER 13:
Be Willing to Take a Risk

You've probably heard this expression: when you continue to do what you've always done, you'll continue to get what you've always gotten. It's a cliché, yet it's true. That's why we already looked at what you can do differently and how you can *be* different. Because that will get you different results.

It's also important to take risks now and then. It can be a financial risk or an emotional one. The kind of risk you need to take is different each time. Some risks feel smaller and others feel bigger. Sometimes taking one risk is all it takes; other times you have to continuously put your ass on the line. The only thing that's certain is that every new goal, dream, or creation requires you to take some kind of risk.

Be willing to take it. It can be tempting to play it safe. But remember, when you continue to do what you've always done, you'll continue to get what you always have gotten.

I'm not suggesting you act irrationally, stupid, or irresponsible. Of course not! I'm talking about doing something that *feels* like a risk, but deep down, you *know* is the right step for you now. Take that risk. Your intuition is always right. What you know deep down is *never* wrong.

REFLECTION

In what ways are you playing it safe instead of doing what you know you have to do?

CHAPTER 14:
Be Willing to Feel Uncomfortable

Most (but not all!!) growth takes place outside of your comfort zone. That's why it feels uncomfortable.

A mistake people often make is to think that feeling uncomfortable is a sign that something is wrong and they need to step back. But you don't have to do that. This unsettling feeling is a sign that you're growing and changing. It's part of the manifestation of your dream. It's part of being in the in-between, in the gap: what you want isn't here yet. You already said good-bye to (parts of) the old you. You're finding your footing in new territory, which doesn't always feel comfortable.

Learn to embrace the discomfort. This doesn't mean you have to like it. It only means you accept it as part of the journey. See it for what it is: a sign that you're growing and transforming. Things are changing. You are changing. Your *life* is changing. And until the *new* has arrived and starts to feel normal, you can experience moments where you feel a bit uneasy. There's nothing wrong with that. It's all part of your journey.

Mind you, sometimes feeling uncomfortable *can* be a sign that something is wrong. How do you know if it's something to accept or if it's a sign something is off? By questioning it. Ask yourself these questions.

- What's going on right now? What exactly am I feeling, and where does that feeling come from?
- What, if anything, do I fear?
- What, if anything, am I resisting?
- Is this the right move and am I just afraid?
- Or is there something wrong?

Ask these questions and notice what feelings and thoughts come up. The answers will tell you if something is wrong, or if you're just getting used to being in unknown territory.

REFLECTION

If you were willing to feel uncomfortable, what would you do today?

How would you show up in a way that is different from how you are now?

CHAPTER 15:
Update Your Self-Image

You grow, learn, and change all the time. You're not the same person you were three years ago. Or even one year ago. But is your self-image up-to-date with the changes you've gone through? Probably not. Your beliefs, actions, circumstances, and results have changed, but this doesn't mean your self-image has automatically upgraded as well. What and how you think about yourself right now is not usually a reflection of who you are TODAY, but of who you were BEFORE. This may hold you back or keep you playing smaller than you're capable of.

So make sure your self-image is up-to-date. It will expand how you think about yourself, make you feel better about yourself, AND get you better results. Here's how you can do that. Look back on the last one to three years and answer the following questions.

What have I learned?

- What new skills have I learned? What knowledge and expertise have I gained?
- What programs did I participate in? What workshops, courses, or events did I attend?
- What books did I read, what coaching did I get, or what mentoring did I receive?
- What has all of this taught me? Make a list of everything you learned.

What successes did I have?

Make a list of every success you had in the past one to three years (in both your business and personal life). Include ALL wins, big and small. After you've completed your list, look at every item and ask yourself these questions.

- What has this success taught me?
- What knowledge have I gained?
- What skills have I learned or developed?
- How has this changed who I am?
- How has this changed what I'm capable of?

What obstacles, doubts, or fears have I overcome?

Look at the things you didn't think you were capable of one to three years ago. What were you scared of? What doubts did you have? How did you overcome them? Write it down, and ask yourself these questions next.

- What has overcoming these fears and doubts taught me?
- How has it changed who I am?
- How has it changed what I'm able to do?
- What is now possible for me that wasn't possible before?

Take some time to make these three lists and answer every question. I guarantee it will make you feel good about yourself! An exercise like this improves your self-esteem. And when you're finished, your self-image will be accurate and up-to-date, which is a real boost for your self-confidence. An updated self-image benefits you greatly in all areas of your life, as well as in manifesting your dreams. Updating your self-image strengthens your certainty that you WILL realize even your biggest projects and goals. This confidence helps you bridge the gap between where you are and where you want to be. Try it!

REFLECTION

If you felt super confident about yourself and your abilities, what would you do today?

How would you show up?

CHAPTER 16:
What It Means to Be Present

Being present means to be fully aware of this moment. To be engaged in this moment. You pay attention to what's in front of you now. You're not thinking about the past or the future. You simply ARE in this moment, and you're absorbed by whatever it is you're doing. It's not a watch-a-movie-and-be-completely-immersed-in-it kind of way. That's more of an escape of your awareness. Instead, you're fully aware of your senses, your body, this entire moment.

For most of us, that's not how we usually go about living our lives. Our attention is normally focused everywhere *but* on this moment. Thankfully, you can learn to be present again. Why should you? When you're present, you have access to your inner stillness, your inner calm. You also have access to all of your power, creativity, and intuition. Your mind is clear. Your body is calm. You feel steady. You're not worried or stressed. Because you feel that in *this* moment, you are okay. And in *this* moment. And in *this* moment.

You only worry or stress when your mind kicks in and starts thinking about the past or the future. When all you can think about is everything you should have done or how much there still is to do. When your mind reels off the things that could go wrong or that aren't already as you want them to be.

In THIS moment, there is no place for any of that. You just *are*. Solutions, insights, big aha moments, intuitive ideas that come to you from out of nowhere . . . They ALL come to you in THIS moment.

This is why you often get great ideas while you're in the shower. You're not thinking about the past or the future. You're just standing there, enjoying the sensation of the water, the soap, the steam, the sounds. You just *are*. You're not trying to find a solution or come up with any ideas. You're just taking a shower. That's all you're doing.

And in that space—the space that opens up because your mind is not preoccupied with the past or the future—ideas, insights, and solutions can come to you. Suddenly you know the title of your blog post or the ending of your book. Suddenly you know which decision to make or how to solve a tricky situation.

When you're present, you're not thinking about how long it will take before your dream will come true or how long you've been working on it already. You're not worrying about it and you're not lost in fears. You just ARE. And in that state of being, that full awareness of this moment, you are fully alive. You know what to do and you know how to be. It's you, this moment, your body, your breath. And in that space, that awareness, everything falls into place. That's what it means to be present. That's why it's so important. And that's why it's the biggest gift you can give yourself.

Being present equals experiencing each moment to its fullest. It's not difficult to be present. But we've all unlearned to just BE. You can relearn how to do it. All it takes is practice, practice, and more practice. The benefits are instant. So give yourself the chance to play with it. The following chapters show you how.

Every moment is a new beginning. Every moment is complete. And in every moment, you are okay, just as you are, wherever you are.

REFLECTION

What would be different if you allowed yourself to be present in each moment, in your body, in each activity?

How would you feel and be different?

How would that make you *feel*?

CHAPTER 17:
Mindfulness Exercise

You may wonder *how* you can be present. An easy and surefire way to bring your awareness back to this moment is by practicing mindfulness. It only takes a minute, and you can do it everywhere, as often as you like.

First, take a couple of deep breaths. Then close your eyes and pay attention to what you hear. From the loudest sounds to the smallest whispers, what do you hear near you and what is in the distance? Don't label, judge, or criticize it. Just notice.

Next, bring your attention to what you see with your eyes closed. Do you see spots and those little squiggly things? Dark and light? Any colors? Again, just notice.

Then, pay attention to what you smell. From the faintest smell to the most noticeable one, far away and up close, be aware of them. Notice without judging or labeling anything.

Next, pay attention to what you feel in your body. Any aches, itches, or pains? Notice every sensation without criticizing or labeling them. Just feel.

Finally, pay attention to what you can taste in your mouth (if anything). Again, just notice.

After you've finished, open your eyes. Be aware of what you can see, hear, feel, smell, and taste now that your eyes are open. And move on with the rest of your day.

You can do this exercise several times per day, in between activities, while you're standing in line, or are stuck in traffic. Without closing your eyes in that last case, of course! Notice the difference in how you feel, in what you do and in how you do it after you practice being present.

REFLECTION

Do this exercise now, before you move on to the next chapter. Try it!

CHAPTER 18:
Breathing

Your breath is a powerful instrument that brings you back to this present moment, back to your body, back to your inner stillness, and back to feeling calm. It's physically impossible to breathe deeply and slowly *and* feel stressed or panic at the same time. Calming your breath always calms *you* down, too.

You can control your breath in several ways. One way is to consciously deepen and slow down the breaths you take. You can do that right now. Inhale deeper and slower than you've done all day. Exhale deeper and slower than you've done all day. Deepen your inhalations and exhalations until you can't breathe in any deeper and slower; let your body take over after that. Let your breath breathe you.

Another way to deepen your breath is to fully *exhale* first. Push out every last bit of air. Your body will automatically take care of a deep inhalation. Sometimes that's an easier way to calm your breath, especially when you feel panicked or stressed. Deepening your inhalations can temporarily feel like your angst is increasing. Focusing first on your exhalation can help.

You can also do this simple breathing exercise. Repeat until you feel calm again: inhale for four counts, hold your breath for four counts, exhale for four counts. Or however many counts feels good to you. As long as your inhalations, exhalations and pauses are equally long.

Your breath is always with you, and you can always practice with deepening it, wherever you are. It's good for your general health, too! Most people breathe too shallowly, so it can't hurt to practice breathing deeper.

REFLECTION

Take a moment now to slow down your breath. If only for three breaths. Notice the difference.

CHAPTER 19:
Meditate

When you're present in this moment you don't think about the past or the future. You're still in the gap between where you are and where you want to be, but it doesn't bother you. You're focused on this moment and this leaves no space to worry about your progress or how long it will take before you achieve your goal.

Your breath and being mindful are wonderful tools to help you be present. So is meditation. You can meditate any way you want: listen to a guided meditation* or you can sit in silence for however long you like. Even five minutes makes a difference. All you have to do is sit, close your eyes, and let your thoughts go by without following them or getting caught up in them. It can help to count your breaths, so you're not focused on your thoughts. Or you can repeat a mantra. Or your own name.

See if you can notice any space between your thoughts. A quiet moment amid those tumbling thoughts. If you can't notice it, that's fine, too. Just sitting and BEing helps you relax and get present.

REFLECTION

Set a timer for thirty seconds. Close your eyes and just BE.

---

* For example, the free app Insight Timer offers excellent guided meditations from different teachers and for different lengths of time.

CHAPTER 20:
Focus on What Feels Good Now

Reflecting on these questions helps you see the beauty that's already in your life and takes your focus away from all the things you haven't achieved yet or aren't happy with.

- What's good in your life right now?
- What's already working?
- What in your life is already the way you want it to be?
- What in your business is already the way you want it to be?
- What's right about this moment?
- What's right about you?

Sure, there's always more to want or to strive for. AND there's always so much to be grateful for, too!

REFLECTION

What would change in your life if you regularly focused on what's already good in your life?

How would focusing on the positive make you feel?

How would it benefit you?

CHAPTER 21:
Follow Your Intuition

You can't always see (or, more accurately, you can rarely see) the path toward your goal. Sure, you can see some steps that will take you there, but the entire path? Especially when your dream or project is big? No. That rarely happens. And on the rare occasion you have everything planned out from start to finish? Plans change. Unexpected things happen. And you need to make adjustments accordingly.

Thankfully, your soul knows how to get you where you want to be. She knows what you want. She knows what you need. She knows your dreams and knows the best way to get there. And she guides you there step-by-step, through your intuition.

Your soul isn't focused only on this one goal you're trying to accomplish. Your soul is holistic: she looks at the *complete* picture of everything that matters to you. She takes your overall health and well-being into consideration, and she combines it all in one big path, where every step you take contributes to at least one thing that matters.

Here's an example of how this works. When she tells you to go to the movies with a friend today, this may be because (a) you need some downtime, (b) you want to have more fun and do more spontaneous things, (c) this movie may inspire an idea for a marketing strategy, (d) you meet your new partner afterward, and / or (e) it takes your mind off of the train of thoughts you've been trapped in for days and opens your mind up for solutions and inspiration.

You don't know why it's a good idea to catch a movie. You don't *have* to know. Your soul knows and that's enough. And she lets you know which step to take through your intuition. Through what you know, deep down, is what you need to do. All you have to do is listen and act upon it.

In every moment, your own inner wisdom tells you exactly what to do. Whether it's taking a nap or having some tea or going to the movies or writing a new sales page: your intuition tells you. All you have to do is follow her guidance.

This guidance isn't always fun, it isn't always easy, and it can feel scary or uncomfortable to follow it. Follow it anyway. It *always* works out for the best, which you know already. I mean, you remember exactly when you ignored it before, right? Those times where you felt something was off, but you ignored the feeling and afterward you always wondered why you didn't listen to your gut feeling. Remember? And I bet you also remember a time where you listened and magic happened—something you wanted somehow fell into your lap.

Listen to your intuition in whatever way it speaks to you. She talks to you in flashes of insight, sudden inspirations, moments of joy and excitement, sensations in your body, and she talks to you through your feelings and emotions, or through a deep down *knowing*.

Listen. Act. Your intuition will bring you what you want and need. It never steers you wrong, and it always knows what to do.

REFLECTION

What does your intuition have to tell you now? Take a moment to deepen your breathing, close your eyes, and ask these questions.

What's the best thing for me to do today?

What's most important for me to focus on now?

Be quiet. Listen. Notice whatever comes up without judging or dismissing it and act on it.

CHAPTER 22:
Relax

One of the biggest shifts I made in my business is a result from something that sounds so simple but is often so hard—to relax. It's something I had to learn. Or rather, I had to UNlearn a lot of things, so that I could sink into relaxation and worry less, while also getting access to all the opportunities, flow, and inspiration that are available 24 −7.

When you feel relaxed you're not worried about the future. You may notice that your dream hasn't manifested yet, but it doesn't bother you. Feeling relaxed and being present go hand in hand. Both help you stay away from worries and stress. And when you feel calm, you're not concerned about being in a gap or being in an in-between phase at all. You just ARE and feel good about it! (Not to mention the benefits that feeling relaxed has for your over-all health and well-being! You feel better and your body functions much better, too. Stress and fear have a huge negative impact on your immune system and fitness!)

These days, I help my clients learn to feel more relaxed, and that process often triggers a lot of questions and resist-ance from them. Here are some examples.

- "But I can't just do NOTHING!"
- "But I have NO TIME to relax!"
- "But if I just sit there and relax, how will I ever get all my shit done?"
- "Yeah, but if I wait until I feel inspired, I won't make any money!"
- "How can I make money if I relax all the time?!"

But feeling relaxed has NOTHING to do with the actions (or lack of actions) you take. Nothing! Relaxation doesn't mean you don't take action. Relaxation is the absence of tension. It truly is! You can be super busy and take five trillion actions every day and feel relaxed the whole time. You can be super lazy and do nothing all day and feel stressed out, guilty, or uncomfortable. You can feel anything BUT relaxed when you're not doing a single thing!

Relaxation is crucial for you, your business, AND for realizing your goals. Because when you're relaxed, you're automatically present in this moment and in your body. You're open to receive opportunities, ideas, insights, inspiration, money, clients, love, joy, pleasure, or anything else you desire. And when you're present, calm, open, and relaxed? Everything flows. You always know what to do. You FEEL GOOD. And the results of your actions are much better, too!

When you think about relaxing in terms of doing less (or even nothing), you may never get around to it. But when you think of relaxing in terms of the absence of tension, you open the door to more inner peace right now.

Tension is triggered by your thoughts and beliefs. Change your thoughts, and you release your tension. Release your tension . . . and you'll relax.

The next time you feel stressed, explore why. What are you thinking that causes you stress? What thoughts make you feel better and release your pressure? Here are some examples.

Thought that causes tension "I should have done more today!"

Thought that releases tension "I did the best I could today." Or "I can't change what I did today. I'll do better tomorrow."

Thought that causes tension "Why is it taking so long?"

Thought that releases tension "I trust everything happens for a reason, even when I don't know what that reason is."

It may take some practice to find a new thought that releases your tension. Play with finding new perspectives anyway. The benefits are HUGE!

In addition, take time to relax. Do things that help you unwind. Do nothing. Even if it's only for a couple of minutes. The more you relax, the better you feel, and the more good things you'll receive. It is worth investing your time and energy into relaxing.

REFLECTION

How could you relax more today?

How and where can you let go of tension right now?

CHAPTER 23:

Move

Work out, take a walk, dance, do yoga, ride your bike. Literally move your body. Anything that moves your body moves your energy, too. Stagnant energy disappears. You feel more energized. Your spirits lift and your mood gets a boost. Crankiness goes away. Moving connects you to your body and you get more grounded and present in this moment, which helps you let go of worries, stress, or impatience. Move. It's good for your body and your mind—and it helps you achieve your goals.

REFLECTION

What does your body need from you now?

How does it want to move?

Let your body show you what (if any) move it wants to make right now, if only to roll your neck or shoulders.

Just feel and follow the movement.

CHAPTER 24:
Surrender & Let Go

Surrendering and letting go does NOT mean that you give up on your dreams. Absolutely not! It only means you give up your need to know what happens next. You let go of your attachment to how or when your dream will come to life. You release your tendency to try to control everything that goes on around you (including others and the universe . . .).

You still want what you want. You still dream. You still have goals. But you don't NEED these things to feel happy or enjoy your life. You can feel happy now. There's always something to enjoy or find pleasure in. There's always something to be grateful for. There are always things that are already good in your life. Your dream is just a new thing to enjoy. But if you can't enjoy the path toward it, you won't feel happy when your dream has come true. Not for long, anyway.

What does it mean if you can't feel happy now? It means that you are overlooking what you have and are focused on what you don't have. It means that you live in the future instead of in this moment. And if you continue to do that, your dream won't make you happy for long—

you'll quickly focus on the next thing you don't have and feel bad about not having that yet.

So surrender. Let go. Let go of your need for things to happen in a certain way or at a certain time. Let go of your need to control. That's fear. The fear that you won't get what you want. The fear that if you're not on it, nothing will happen. But that's not true. You're not in this alone. The manifestation and realization of your goals is a creation among you and your soul, the universe, life itself. You decide what you want and take the actions you need to. (How you know which actions these are? Your intuition tells you.) Everything else? It's up to the universe. You have no control over that. And that's a good thing! Because the universe knows EVERYTHING. It has unlimited power, unlimited possibilities, unlimited abundance, and infinite intelligence. It creates stars and moons and galaxies and all of life. Don't you think that offers a few more options than you can come up with yourself?

All you have to do is know what you want. Choose it. Decide. Take the actions you need to. And let go of the rest. Do your thing and then focus on what the next moment brings you. Allow the universe to handle the rest. Let it surprise and delight you. Let its magic work for you while you focus on whatever this moment wants from you. When you do that, impatience disappears. You stop thinking about how long it will take or if you'll ever get what you want. You just ARE. You live, breathe, and enjoy each moment as best you can.

REFLECTION

What are you holding onto?

What outcomes are you attached to?

What would happen if you surrendered and let go of that attachment now?

How would it feel to let go?

CHAPTER 25:
See It as a Done Deal

When you're in the gap you can get stuck in hoping or wishing that what you want might show up some day. But there's no power in wishing or hoping. Instead, see it as already yours. That energy has power, trust, and decisiveness in it. It's like ordering something online: it's not here yet, but you know you will have it. It may take a day or there may be a delay. Something may go wrong or you may need to contact customer service, but the thing you ordered WILL arrive on your doorstep. It's not here yet, but it's already yours.

Treat your dreams and goals the same way. See them as a done deal. They haven't shown up in your reality yet, but they will!

REFLECTION

If your dream were already here, it's yours, and it's a done deal, what would you do today?

How would you act?

How would you feel?

What would you do today if you trusted it's a given that your dream comes true?

CHAPTER 26:
Good Self-Care

Take excellent care of yourself. Eat healthy, sleep well, move your body, drink enough water. Be kind to yourself, prioritize your well-being, and do whatever helps you keep your energy high. It's good for you and helps you realize your dreams. You have less energy when you don't take good care of yourself. You're less creative. You have less space to focus on your dreams.

Good self-care benefits you in all areas of your life, on every level.

REFLECTION

What do you need right now?

What does your soul need?

What does your body need?

How can you take excellent care of yourself today?

CHAPTER 27:
Be Okay with Not Knowing

I know. You want to know it all, don't you? You want to know how much longer you have to wait and what will happen next and why someone isn't returning your call and how is it possible that the universe is infinite?! That boggles your mind every time you think about it.

You just want to *know*. But you don't know everything. You don't always know what to do. You don't always see the answer to your question. You don't always see the big picture. (In fact, you rarely do.) And you don't always understand why things are the way they are or why people do what they do.

But there's power in *not* knowing. When you accept that you don't know something, you are open. Open to receive answers and guidance. Open to think differently and come up with creative ideas. Your quest for knowledge and answers can take you away from what's in front of you now.

Everything you need to know right now is exactly what you know right now. Everything you don't know yet? You don't need to know now or at all.

REFLECTION

How would you feel if you trusted that you don't need to know whatever it is that you don't know yet?

What if you stopped looking for answers and trusted they will come to you when you're ready?

What could that trust bring you?

CHAPTER 28:
Full Acceptance

If there's one big energy drain and one incredibly frustrating—and unproductive—habit, it's this: resisting or fighting the way things are.

You can still want things to be different! But that won't change the way things are in this moment. You can take action so something changes in the (near) future. But that won't change how things are right now. It's pointless to fight how something *is* now, because it won't change this moment. Fighting takes your energy and attention away from what you could be doing to create something different in the next moment.

Let me give you some examples to clarify what this means. Let's say that you're hungry. You sit on the couch and you're famished. You don't like that feeling. You want food! You get angry at being hungry. You resent it. You don't want to feel it any longer! Why do you have to feel hungry to begin with?! It's so annoying! You get worked up about it. All you can think about is wolfing down a burger. But you don't have a burger! You resist your craving, but it won't go away! It only gets worse.

Fighting that feeling doesn't change a thing. Your hunger won't go away unless you eat something. Fighting your feeling doesn't feed you. Eating an apple does.

Or let's say that it's raining. You don't want that. You don't like it. You were all set to go to the beach, and that plan has now gone down the drain. You really craved a sunny day and a dip in the sea, but there is no sun and you hate to swim when it's pouring. You can resist and fight it all you want. But that won't bring out the sun. In fact, there's absolutely NOTHING *you* can do to bring out the sun. Fighting the rain makes you cranky, and it costs you a ton of energy. But it's not until you let go of your resistance that you can see other options and enjoy your day off.

The same principle applies to every situation you are in: the more you fight it, the more energy you lose. The worse you feel. And the fewer opportunities you see to create change. It's only when you stop fighting and you accept what IS, in THIS moment, that you're open and able to see options to create change for the NEXT moment.

Whether you're impatient because your dream hasn't been realized yet or it's raining or your bank account is almost empty, in THIS moment, it is what it is. It can change. It *will* change. Your situation might not change in an instant. But how you *feel* about your situation can change in a matter of seconds!

Change can happen when you fully accept whatever IS in this moment and what WAS in the past. It is what it is. Don't attach any meaning or story to the way things are or have been. Because giving it meaning is usually what makes you feel bad. It just IS. By accepting the past, you bring your attention back to this present moment, giving you access to your full energy, power, and creativity to change what you want to change—starting with your mood. Once you stop resisting and start accepting, your mood lifts and your energy returns.

What if you stopped fighting what IS and focus on what COULD be instead? What if the way things are means nothing more and nothing less than that: this is just how things are in this moment. And they can and *will* change. Nothing lasts forever. Including this moment. And this one. Everything always changes. This too will change. This too shall pass. All you have to do is say, "Okay, this is how it is. Now what? What's next? What would I like to see instead? And what can I do about that now?"

REFLECTION

What are you resisting?

What could happen if you stopped fighting that?

PART TWO:

TIPS & INSPIRATION TO STAY MOTIVATED

INTRODUCTION

It can sometimes feel like you'll be in the gap between where you are and where you want to be forever. But you won't. This in-between phase is only temporary, I promise!

The following chapters give you tips and inspiration that help you move through this phase with as much ease as possible. Some chapters help you identify where you might feel stuck and show you how to break through that.

Your goals and dreams WILL come true for you one day. Until that moment is there, this part of the book helps you trust that all is well and life will only get better!

CHAPTER 1:
Make Sure You REALLY Want It

You'll never stay motivated for a goal or dream you don't TRULY want. So before you read ANY of the next chapters, check if you're chasing your true dream or not.

You can check it by asking yourself this question: if anything is possible, if I feared nothing, and if I trusted that everything always works out for me perfectly, what would I want? Is this it? Or would I want something different?

If you're still passionate about your dream, you're free to move forward. But if you're not, it's time to tweak your dream. If you feel there's nothing you can do to fall back in love with it, it's time to pursue a new dream instead.

REFLECTION

Do your current goals and dreams represent what you TRULY want? Or do they reflect what you think you can get?

If you find you're not sure what you truly want, check out my book *Unmute Your Life - break free from fear and go for what you REALLY want.* That helps you clarify *and* realize your true dreams. You can read all about it here: www.unmuteyourlife.com

CHAPTER 2:
Divine Timing

It's only human to want everything now, or at least quickly. Sometimes things do happen quickly. But sometimes . . . it takes longer than you'd like. And there's only so much you can do about that. Because there's more than just your timing, there's divine timing, too: the time something takes—without you being able to influence it—for reasons that aren't always clear.

Things take as long as they take. Which can be incredibly frustrating. Believe me—I know. But in EVERY process of creation that's just how it is. A healthy pregnancy takes nine months, regardless of how long YOU want it to take. You can eat healthy, work out, and get enough sleep—and it still takes nine months. You can visualize it taking less time and open your mind to the possibility of giving birth to a healthy baby after two months—yet it still takes nine months. You can work with mantras, burn incense, and create vision boards, and it still takes nine months. You can be in a hurry and try to will it to go faster, or get angry, or beg, or cry, or hope all you want, and it still takes nine months . . .

This is true for EVERY goal, dream, or creation: it takes as long as it takes. I'm repeating that in the hope it sinks in. Because with *everything* you create, there is your timing . . . and there's divine timing. You can't make anything go faster than it's destined to take. You have no control over it. And you have no idea how long something will take, why that's the case, or who decides it.

I've seen over and over how trying to force things to go faster doesn't work. Sure, sometimes you can speed things up. You can work harder or do more, but that only gets you so far. After that, it's out of your hands again.

Taking the actions that are yours to take, at the moment you're supposed to take them: *this* is what's in your hands. These are your inspired actions—the actions your intuition tells you to take. The actions that deep down you *know* are the right actions for you. Taking these actions is all that is completely in your power to do. After that, you have no control over the timing. Now it takes as long as it takes. Which can take longer than you hope. But it can also go much faster than you can imagine! That's why it's important to stay open and unattached to what happens after you've done your thing. There's a lot of freedom in knowing (and especially *accepting*) that every manifestation has its own timing. It releases you from the stress and pressure of trying to make shit happen and thinking you can control the universe. Sure, we all have fantasies about how great it would be if we were the master of the universe. Well, at least I do. :-) But would that *really* be so great? Are you sure?

There is beauty, magic, and relief in knowing you're not the only one involved in *any* manifestation process. The entire power and wisdom of the universe are both part of your creation. And the universe brings resources and magic to the table that your mind cannot grasp.

There's a perfect timing for everything. And *you* don't have to know what it is. Yes, sometimes that pisses you off and it's annoying as hell. And sometimes . . . you realize the perfection of it.

So do what you need to do and let go after that. If things move more quickly than you expected, move along with it. If things go slower than you hoped, move along with it. Do what you can and leave it at that. Trust the flow of life. Trust the flow of whatever it is you're working on. Don't give up and don't force what's not ready. Use the inspiration and exercises from this book to help you stay true to that flow, to that rhythm you can't see or touch but that's always working with you, working *for* you.

Trust divine timing. And trust your own inner wisdom and intuition to show you when to act and when to let go. It always tells you. All you have to do is listen.

REFLECTION

If you fully trusted that everything would unfold for you in the perfect right time, in the perfect right way, what would you do?

What would you let go of?

How would you feel?

CHAPTER 3:

Choose to Trust

If you don't trust that you're capable of reaching your goals, this means you believe that you're not able to. If you don't trust that you can make money doing what you love, this means you believe that you can't. If you don't trust your intuition, this means you believe it will steer you wrong.

What *do* you trust about realizing your dreams? Do you trust that you're capable of manifesting them? That you're worthy of receiving what you want? That it's possible for you to reach higher and succeed? That it will be fun to shoot for the moon and land somewhere beautiful?

Or . . .

Do you trust that you're incapable, unworthy, and destined to play small? That what you want will always remain just outside your reach? That maaayyyyybe you can create a different life for yourself, but it will be hard and take forever and will require many compromises and sacrifices along the way?

You always trust *something*. Put your trust in something that serves you. You probably can't shift your mind from believing that you're incapable to believing that you're gifted. That's too big a leap to take at once. But maybe you can trust that you're more capable than you think. That you can learn to open up to receive more. Maybe you can trust that your journey could be easier and you might learn to relax—if only a little more. Maybe you can trust that you're able to change, to grow, and to be surprised at what's possible for you.

Here are some questions you can ask yourself to start practicing what you choose to trust.

- What areas in your life would benefit from a shift in trust?
- How would that shift make you feel different?
- What would you do differently if you trusted that everything always works out for you perfectly?
- And what could believing in that possibly open up for you?

It may seem that the shift is tiny. And it is. But tiny is NOT the same as insignificant. On the contrary! The effects can be HUGE.

Shifting what you put your trust in changes EVERYTHING. Shifting from believing that I was incapable and too scared to trusting that I could grow and take steps despite being afraid helped me to start my business, to write my first book, to work globally—it helped me do about 95% of EVERYTHING I do in my business today.

The same is true for you. You wouldn't have achieved or changed ANYTHING in your life if you didn't have at least *some* faith in yourself and what you can do.

A little trust is all you need. Choose to trust that you can change and grow. Choose to trust that everything works out for you, always. Choose to trust that your dream will unfold and you'll achieve all your goals.

REFLECTION

If you fully trusted yourself and life, what would today look like?

What would you do?

How would you feel?

CHAPTER 4:
Look for the Evidence

What you focus on is what you'll see more of. Use that principle to your benefit by looking for the evidence that what you want is on its way to you. That it's unfolding for you now. That (some of) it is here already.

The evidence is always there. Sometimes in the form of tangible proof. Sometimes in the form of how you feel. And sometimes you need a little creativity to find the evidence. Let's say you want to make more money. Here are some examples of evidence that money is on its way to you.

- You found money on the street.
- Someone bought one of your products.
- A happy client referred someone to you. (Who may or may not buy from you, but it's a possibility.)
- You feel more positive about money.
- You got a discount at the drugstore, etc.

Look for evidence every week. If this exercise speaks to you and makes you feel better about reaching your goal, by all means, do it daily!

If it doesn't speak to you OR it forces you to focus only on what you DON'T have, skip it. It's a powerful exercise, but it doesn't work for everyone. It works like a charm for me now, but when I first practiced with looking for evidence, it didn't. It made me feel worse! It made me realize that I did NOT have what I wanted yet. I was too attached to my goal. So I stopped doing this exercise and focused on things that helped me relax and feel good.

On other occasions, I have benefited immensely from this exercise. For me, it works especially well in situations where I want to change how I feel, or if I want to experience more of a specific feeling. For example, I used this exercise to feel safer about making myself visible. Every day I wrote down three pieces of evidence that showed me it was safe to be (more) visible. I sent out a newsletter and still felt good. I posted something scary on Facebook and nothing bad happened. I made a video and even received a compliment for it!

I also used it to learn to relax more. Every day, I wrote down three pieces of evidence that showed me being relaxed also benefited my business. One time, a client signed up while I was sleeping. One time, I sold a product while I was having a massage. One time, people signed up for my list while I was sailing. I've sold books without doing any marketing for them. I continued to collect evidence until I felt I no longer needed it: I fully believed it was safe to relax.

You can stop collecting evidence the moment you notice your belief has shifted. You know you no longer need it when your evidence begins to feel normal to you. Of course someone signed up for your program when you were asleep! Clients always come to you when you relax. Of course you found money on the street! Money flows to you always without you doing anything special for it. Once you notice thoughts like these, you know your belief has shifted and you can stop doing this exercise.

These examples may not resonate with you at all, and that's fine; it's all about what works for YOU. What YOU see as evidence. Again, it's okay to be creative. I recently asked the universe to bring me a shitload of money, please and thank you very much. Five minutes later I opened my e-mail and found one of these spam emails with the wonderful news that I had inherited a couple of million dollars from someone I didn't know, but somehow, they knew of me and wanted to give me a big chunk of cash after they passed. :-) No, it's not real money, and yes, it was obviously a scam. But to me, it still counts as evidence.

Last word on this tool: it's okay to repeat the same evidence. It's not so much about what you write down but about *how it makes you feel.* The point of this exercise is that it makes you excited about whatever it is you want, you learn to trust that it's available to you, and it helps you feel confident that what you want is on its way to you now—it is here for you already!

REFLECTION

Where can you already see evidence that what you want is on its way to you?

Reflect on it and take a moment to feel grateful and happy about your progress!

CHAPTER 5:

You Can Have What
You Want Now

You can have what you want now. That may sound weird in a book about bridging the gap between where you are and where you want to be. The gap implies that what you want is not here yet.

But the thing is, BOTH statements are true at the same time.

What you want is not here yet.

AND

You can have what you want now.

How is that possible? Because the actual *thing* you desire may not be here yet, but you can experience the *feeling* it will bring you now. Here's an example to clarify what that means.

Let's say it's your desire to write and publish a book. You think the feeling of seeing your book in print will bring you deep satisfaction. Your book is not here yet. But that feeling is available to you now. You can feel satisfied this moment. You can recall a time you felt deep satisfaction and feel that again now. You can also ask yourself what would give you a feeling of satisfaction today and do whatever will make you feel that way.

Another example is starting your own business. You want to be your own boss because you think you will experience more freedom. Your business is not here yet. But you can feel more free right now. Recall a time you felt free, and feel that feeling course through your body. Ask yourself what would make you feel free today and act on the answers you get. That's how you can get what you want *now* without actually having the thing you desire yet.

Play with it! Not only will it make you feel better, it ALSO helps you to manifest your goal or dream with more ease, and perhaps even more quickly. What you focus on expands, and what you give your attention to is what you'll experience more of. If you focus on what you want to feel, you'll attract more things that make you feel that way into your life—including the fulfillment of your goal.

REFLECTION

What is it you desire?

How do you think it will make you feel once you have that?

How could you experience more of that feeling today?

What would make you feel that way now?

How can you add more of that feeling to everything you do?

CHAPTER 6:
Change Can Happen Fast

People often think change takes a long time. Or that certain things need to happen BEFORE what they want can come to them. Maybe you think that, too. Maybe you think the unfolding of your dream will take at least six more months, or any other measure of time. Or maybe you think that your whole mindset needs to shift and all your fears need to be gone before you can see the results you're after.

In business, I've seen a lot of this-before-that thinking in my clients AND myself. (Sometimes I still think that one thing needs to happen before another can happen. Which *can* be true . . . but often isn't.) Here are some common examples of a this-before-that mindset in business. You may find yourself thinking things like this.

- You can't find clients before your website is up.
- Your website can't go up before you have a logo or a professional headshot.
- You can't sell anything if you don't do any marketing.

- You need to have a catchy one-liner that perfectly describes what you do before you can make more money.
- You won't be able to get more clients until your sales page / about page / website is revamped.
- Your e-mail list can't grow until you have the perfect gift.
- You can't start a blog until you know all the ins and outs of having a blog, etc.

When it comes to realizing dreams, especially big ones, it's easy to think so much needs to happen before that dream can come to life. Maybe that's true. But maybe it isn't. If you think it will take a long time or other things need to happen BEFORE you can reach your goal, it will probably take a while. What you expect to see is what you *will* see. There may be golden opportunities under your nose right now without you seeing or recognizing them. You aren't expecting them—so it's easy to overlook them.

You don't know how long it will take to realize your dream. It can take longer than you think, it can happen faster than you believe is possible, and it can even happen NOW.

Keep the door open. Let go of any expectations or neediness around *when* your dream might be realized. By keeping an open mind, you leave space for a quicker, easier manifestation than your limited mind can imagine. The universe has tricks up its sleeve that you have no idea of. :-) The more open you are to how fast things can go, the faster things can go. The less you resist what's happening and how it happens, the easier your dreams can unfold. The less you resist, the more open you are to seeing options and opportunities that are already available to you this minute.

REFLECTION

If you fully trusted that change can happen fast, what would be different for you today?

How would you feel different?

How would you act differently?

CHAPTER 7:
Manifestation Can Be Instant

The idea that manifestation can be instant is more or less the same message as that of the previous chapter, *Change Can Happen Fast*. But *fast* still implies that a certain length of time must pass between knowing what you want and seeing it show up in your reality. And I'd like you to keep your mind as open as possible to how things can unfold without you being attached to the *how* or the *when*. Because the more open you are to how good things can be, the better they can get.

This is why I'd like to remind you that manifestation doesn't always need time. Manifestation can be (pretty) instant. Things you want or need can show up this moment, this day, within twenty-four hours, or thirty minutes from now. I'm sure you've experienced it before. You may not have consciously registered it, or you considered it a fluke, a coincidence, or a stroke of dumb luck. But it was instant manifestation. It's a thing. It's real. It has happened to you before. And it can happen again. And again. And again.

You may not be convinced yet, so I'll give you some examples to jog your memory. You thought about buying a new car, and that same day a friend calls and tells you they're thinking about selling their car. You love their car and a deal is made within minutes. Or maybe you were the one who wanted to sell the car and hoped you could sell it fast and with no hassle. Ta-da! Instant manifestation.

Maybe you thought it would be great if there was a cookbook with gluten-free cake recipes, and you get one as a gift that same day. Or you see an ad for one when you open the newspaper one minute after you thought this.

Maybe you thought it would be cool if someone bought one of your workshops today, only to open your in-box two seconds later and what do you know: one workshop sold.

Manifestation can be instant. What you want can show up for you NOW. Whether it's a *big* thing or a *small* thing. That might make a difference to you, but it doesn't make a difference to the universe.

REFLECTION

How would you feel if you believed manifestation can be instant?

What could open up for you then?

CHAPTER 8:

What You Want Is on Its Way to You Now

Sometimes it seems like everything is standing still. Like *you* are standing still.

Know that this is never the case. It *feels* that way! But it's never true. Every creation has phases where change is visible. You take actions; you see results; your circumstances change. And every creation has phases where nothing seems to happen. BOTH phases are part of EVERY creation.

Sometimes you need time to heal or to integrate previous learnings or shifts. Sometimes you need rest, so your body can catch up with the changes you went through on a spiritual, mental, and emotional level. Sometimes new ideas or insights need to percolate and brew. Sometimes you need to let go of old stuff and work through old emotions before something new can come into your life. And sometimes you need to learn or experience something before you're ready to move forward. These reasons require a pause.

Whatever the reason may be, there's always *something* happening when things seem to go slow. It's never a mistake. It always happens for your benefit and it always contributes to your journey.

Manifestation happens partially in the physical realm where you can take actions and see tangible results. And part of it—maybe even most of it—happens in the invisible realm, in the invisible energy. Remind yourself of this when it seems like you're standing still. There's a reason for this pause. Whatever that reason is, it serves you. And even though you may not *see* any progress or change, that doesn't mean it's absent!

There's SO much more to life than meets the eye. What you think of as reality is only a projection of your consciousness and is just a small part of life. You have no idea what's happening behind the scenes for you!

What you want is on its way to you now. Whether or not you can see it. Remind yourself of that and then let go. Bring your attention back to this moment. Find joy in this moment. And before you know it, you'll see the results you've been waiting for.

REFLECTION

If you trusted that what you want is on its way to you now, what would you do today?

How would you feel and act differently?

CHAPTER 9:
Why It Will All Work Out

It's easy to get lost in thoughts about why something might not work or will not happen. But thoughts like that aren't helpful and only bring you down. If you notice that you are doubtful that everything will work out, it's time to shift your focus. These journaling questions help. Answer all of them or pick one that speaks to you.

- Why will it all work out perfectly for you?
- Why are you capable of realizing this dream?
- Why is it IMpossible for this dream to NOT come true?
- Why can this dream easily come true?
- Why is it impossible for you to fail?
- Why is success inevitable for you?

Be open. Be creative. Be curious. Don't worry if your answers *seem* unrealistic. You have *no* idea what's possible or what's realistic. Miracles happen. And things can work out better and easier than you think!

REFLECTION

What would today look like if you trusted that everything would always work out for you and with ease?

What would you do?

How would you feel?

CHAPTER 10:

Feed Your Dreams, Not Your Fears

You can feed either your dreams or your fears. If you don't consciously pay attention to what you think about, your mind drifts off into the negative pretty quickly, which isn't strange at all. Our built-in survival instincts are programmed to scan the world for danger and threats. This makes sense, because our instincts want to keep us safe and for us to survive. We're often told to avoid anything that could be scary or unsafe and to calculate our risks. Our default behavior is driven by our need to avoid our fears and avoid risks. We call that facing reality.

But that's not the only reality. We're souls having a human experience and our possibilities are unlimited. It's just our minds that are limited. And left to its own devices, the mind turns to negative thoughts.

Thankfully, we can retrain our minds. Practice by being curious, having an open mind, expecting the best, and focusing on your well-being and dreams. You do that by constantly bringing your attention back to your dream and consciously feeding your dream.

How? Focus on how your dream makes you feel. Focus on your excitement and curiosity. Remind yourself why you want it and why it matters to you. Remind yourself how amazing it will be to have it.

If you like, you can create a vision board as a reminder of your dream and how it makes you feel. Hang it on your wall or use it as your screensaver on your laptop and phone. You can visualize what it's like to live your dream and imagine how it feels. You can journal about already having it, or about how easy and fun the journey will be, or about how good it can get.

You can use any of these tools I mention. They all work.

All that *really* matters is to train yourself to focus on your dreams instead of on your fears, to spend more time thinking about the positives of your dream instead of the negatives of your fear, to expect good instead of bad, to hope instead of worry.

You can start right now. Think about your dream or goal. Remind yourself why you want it. Remind yourself how it will feel to achieve it. *Feel* this for a couple of seconds, maybe even a minute, before you turn to the next chapter. That's all. That's how easy it is to feed your dream.

REFLECTION

Today, if you were to feed your dreams instead of your fears, what would that look like? What would you do?

What wouldn't you do?

How would you act and show up?

CHAPTER 11:

Enjoy the Moment

You want what you want because you think it will make you happy. That's why you dream. That's why you set goals. Ultimately, you just want to be happy. So why not take the shortcut and be happy NOW?

By all means, have dreams, goals, visions, and aspirations. ENJOY each moment as best you can, too. Happiness is not a destination. It's something you can *only* feel in the present moment. You can only be happy NOW. By enjoying each moment as much as you can, you are happier already. By being happier right now, the journey toward the realization of your dream is much more enjoyable, too!

REFLECTION

What would make you happy now?

What would bring you joy today?

Do that.

CHAPTER 12:

Look at Where You're Going, Not Where You Came From

When you're in the gap your thoughts often switch between the past and the future. One moment you can wonder why you left what you know behind you, and the next you wonder how long it will take before your goal is finally realized. Thoughts like these can make this phase between where you are and where you want to be painful or hard.

The solution is to stay present in this moment and to look forward to what's coming with excitement and curiosity. Stop looking back. Backward is not where you're going. It's only a distraction. The more you look at where you came from, the longer you stay there. The more you look at where you're going, the easier it is to recognize the actions you need to take and the opportunities that will get you there.

Keep your eye on your dream, your goal, your future, while being present in this moment. I know this may sound confusing and contradictory, but it isn't. You're present in this moment. But while you are, you still think thoughts.

You're never *not* thinking. Make sure your thoughts revolve around where you're going and how you choose to feel.

Your thoughts determine how you feel and which actions you take. So keep them focused on where you're going instead of where you came from. This helps you make decisions and take actions that move you forward instead of keeping you where you are.

REFLECTION

What can you do today that brings you closer to your dream?

CHAPTER 13:

(Re)connect with Your Dream

If you've been working on reaching your dream or goal for a while, it can start to feel stale. You can lose touch with your enthusiasm and excitement—which makes it harder to stay motivated and remain committed to doing whatever is needed to realize your desire.

Keep the fire of your dream burning. It's still there! You just need a reminder of it now and then. Remind yourself by answering these questions.

- Why do you want this?
- Why does this goal or dream matter to you?

Write down twenty-five reasons why this goal is important to you. I know that sounds like a lot. But writing down this many reasons connects you to the deeper motivation underneath your dreams. *That's* where your true passion lies.

Wake up that passion regularly. Feel your excitement and your joy, and relish in them. Waking up your passion makes you feel good, and it revitalizes you and your dream. It makes life fun again!

REFLECTION

What excites you the most about your goal or dream? *Feel* this excitement now.

CHAPTER 14:

Do Something Every Day

Keep your goal or dream alive by checking in on it every day. Ask yourself, what can I do today that brings me closer to the manifestation of my dream?

Be quiet and pay close attention to the answers that come up. Notice the little nudges, the tiny niggles, and pay attention to what you know, deep down, to be right.

This doesn't mean you need to take *action* every day (or even at all!!). Taking breaks, relaxing, having fun—they're all important parts of realizing your goals. Of LIFE.

You don't have to check in on your dream every day to realize it. You can manifest what you want without doing that. But it can help! We've all been conditioned to think that to *achieve* something, we must take *action*. Most of us are more focused on *doing* than on *being*. But manifestation starts on the inside: your energy, your awareness, your consciousness—these are what create and manifest your results. Your actions are sometimes necessary, but not always. That's not what we have learned about how the world operates, so it can be hard to let go of the need to DO something and to let go of the idea that results require action.

Tuning into your dream every day gives you the impression of taking action, of DOING something to manifest your goal, which puts your rational mind at ease: oh, right, yep, all is well, she's *doing* shit, that's good, we don't have to kick her in the butt then.

Tune into your dream when it feels good. Don't do it when it doesn't. This goes for EVERYTHING I write in this book. :-) What doesn't feel good never works for you; what feels good always does.

I repeat this idea in the next chapter, in case you skip around the book and don't read every chapter. Because it may well be the most important thing to take away from this book.

REFLECTION

What can you do today that brings you closer to realizing your dream?

If you fully believed your dream WILL come true for you, what would you do today?

Do that.

CHAPTER 15:
Do What Feels Good

Whatever feels *genuinely* good to you works for you. What doesn't feel good to you doesn't. Keep that in mind for everything you read in this book, for everything you read and hear, for any advice anyone gives you, or for whatever someone tells you. Does it feel good to you? Do it. It will work for you. Does it make you feel bad? Don't do it. It won't work for you. This is true for marketing strategies, business building tools, achieving your goals, realizing your dreams, and life itself.

Yes, everything I write in this book works. Not everything I've written about will work best for *you*. I can't be the judge of what works for you, only YOU can be the judge of what works for you. So pay attention to how you feel. If you think you need to take certain actions to get the results you want, but these actions make you feel bad—don't take them. Either explore what makes you feel bad and change your thoughts and beliefs until it feels good or don't take that action at all.

Something that feels good meets no resistance, which leaves you open to receive what you want.

Something that feels bad triggers resistance, which closes you off from receiving what you want.

So focus on what feels good and spend more time on those things. Eliminate what doesn't feel good by changing what you do **OR** by changing what you think, feel, and believe about what you're doing. When you do that, from then on, it'll be smoother sailing in all areas of your life.

REFLECTION

What feels genuinely good to you now? Do that.

CHAPTER 16:
Go Back to the Original Inspiration

Sometimes working on your goal can feel like a chore: there's no juice or joy behind it anymore.

Sometimes your goal feels complicated. You get lost in how to get there or in details that aren't important. You overthink and it feels like a drag instead of an exciting journey.

When this happens, you need to go back to your original inspiration. To the moment your idea first hit, you were excited, and you felt like it was the best idea you've ever had. That moment before you started worrying or fears kicked in.

Go back to the time your dream was born: when the spark hit; when it felt so right; when it brought you joy; when it felt so expansive, so good.

Remember that?

Seriously. Take a moment to remember that now. To really FEEL and enjoy it!

REFLECTION

What was it that excited you about your goal or dream when you first had it?

Can you remember that excitement now?

CHAPTER 17:

Most Importantly

The most important thing to remember and do is to bring your attention back to the present moment. To do what's in front of you now. To enjoy this moment as best you can.

When you do what's in front of you now, there is never any gap. When you enjoy each moment as best you can, your life is filled with more happiness and light.

If this is the only thing you take away and implement from this book, you're all set for life. :-)

REFLECTION

What requires your attention right now?

What wants to be done or expressed through you right now?

What does this moment call far?

And how can you most enjoy that?

CHAPTER 18:
Get Support

If you find it hard to stay positive, or if you struggle, or if you feel stuck along the way: get support. Hire a coach, ask a friend to help you, or find an accountability partner. If it's hard for you to do it on your own, then don't. There are people who can help you, support you, guide you, and cheer you on. You do everything yourself, but you don't have to do it alone. Why would you if you're having a hard time realizing your dream? Why would you risk not realizing your dream OR why would you make your journey harder by doing it alone?

I've always hired coaches or joined courses and done programs to help me and to make my journey easier and more fun. Sometimes I arrange other forms of support from friends or fellow entrepreneurs. It makes my life simpler, more pleasant, and more fun. I always do everything my way, and I do lots of things alone. But if it can be effortless, fun, and save me time? I'm IN, baby. :-)

It's an act of self-love and self-care to allow yourself to get support. Paid or unpaid, professional support or that of a friend, it doesn't matter. There's always help available, as long as you're open and willing to receive it, ask for it, and invest in it.

If you don't need it and feel good about your journey, don't bother and continue to do what you're doing. No need to mess with what works.

But if you'd like your journey to be smoother, you have questions you can't find answers to, or you wonder if there's an easier, faster way to get what you want? Get support.

REFLECTION

Where are you struggling, feeling alone, or putting in more effort than you'd like?

What if it could be easier, faster, less lonely, or less painful?

What could help?

Who could help?

And what will you do about that today?

WHAT'S NEXT?

I hope this book helps you manifest all your dreams, goals, and aspirations.

If you're looking for more inspiration or support, I've got you covered!

First, check www.gapbookgift.com for complimentary gifts, including a master class, a collection of reflections, and an article on why it took me nine years to write my book *Unmute Your Life*, and more information about what you can learn from my journey.

Check out my online program The Gap at www.program-thegap.com if you'd like to dive deeper into what you learned in this book and get my support in bridging the gap.

You can find my other books, programs and coaching at www.programsandmore.com.

Thank you for reading and playing with this book. I hope you enjoyed it and if so, please leave me a brilliant review! Or just a nice one. That'll make me happy, too. :-)

For now, I wish you all the best, and good luck with realizing your goals and dreams!

Love,

Brigitte